A Sense of Science
Exploring Plants

Claire Llewellyn

W
FRANKLIN WATTS
LONDON • SYDNEY

First published in 2007 by
Franklin Watts
338 Euston Road
London NW1 3BH

Franklin Watts Australia
Level 17/207 Kent Street
Sydney NSW 2000

Editor: Jeremy Smith
Art Director: Jonathan Hair
Design: Matthew Lilly
Cover and design concept:
Jonathan Hair

Photograph credits:
Steve Shott except:
istockphoto: 6,
9b, 10b, 11b,
14, 15t, 16-17
all, 24-25 all.
Corbis: 11t.

A CIP
catalogue
record for this
book is available
from the British
Library.

Dewey classification: 580

ISBN: 978 0 7496 7047 4

Printed in China

Franklin Watts is a division of
Hachette Childrens's Books.

Contents

A world of plants

Plants grow all around us.

They grow in parks and gardens.

They grow along
paths and pavements.

Plant spotter
Have a look
outside your home
or school. Where
can you spot plants
growing?

Some plants
grow in water.

All kinds of plants

There are all sorts of different plants.

A buttercup is a small, colourful plant.

Feel it

Look closely at the trunks of three different trees. Do they look and feel the same?

Trees are tall and woody.

Seaweed is flat and rubbery.

Cacti are spiky.

The parts of a plant

Plants are made
up of different parts.

Flower

Leaf

Stem

Roots

They have roots,
a stem and leaves.
Many have flowers, too.

A sunflower has a very tall stem.

I spy
Look at a plant growing in the ground. Which parts of it can you see? Which parts can't you see? Why?

A plant's roots grow under the ground.

Looking at leaves

Most plants have green leaves.
They come in many shapes and sizes.

Some plants
lose their leaves
in the winter.

Dead or alive

Find a dead leaf on the ground. How is it different from a leaf that is growing on a plant?

Some plants keep their leaves all the year round.

Looking at flowers

Many plants
grow flowers.

Sniff, sniff

Go outside and sniff
some flowers. Do they
all have a sweet smell?

Petal

Most flowers
have colourful
petals and a sweet smell.

When the petals fall off, the flowers grow into fruits.

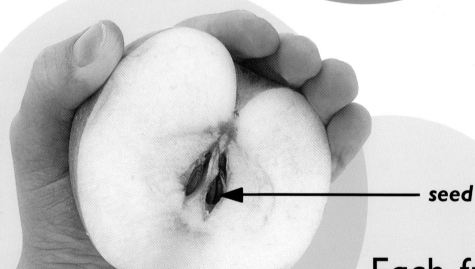

seed

Each fruit has seeds inside.

A plant grows

Most plants
grow from seeds.

A pea seed
sprouts when it is
warm and damp

Day 1
A pea seed

Day 7
The seed
grows a
root and
a tiny shoot.

Shoot

Root

Is it a pea?
How is the pea seed in the picture different from the peas we eat?

Leaves

Stem

Day 21
The pea plant grows bigger. It has leaves and a stem now.

Roots

Plants and water

Plants need water to grow.

Always wash your hands after touching the soil.

Their roots suck up water from the soil.

This plant has died because it had no water.

Wet and dry
What does soil feel like when it is wet? What does it feel like when it is dry?

Rain helps plants to grow.

Plants and light

Plants need light to grow. The light comes from the Sun.

This plant has been growing in the light.

Spot the difference
What differences do you notice between these two plants?

This plant has been growing in the dark.

Eating plants

Plants give us food
to eat. They give us fruits,
vegetables and seeds.

Fruit and veg

Have a look at some fruit and vegetables.
With an adult, cut them up. How do they
look, feel, smell and taste?

Farmers grow plants for us to eat.

Orange juice,
cornflakes,
bread, jam…
many different
foods are made
from plants.

Food for animals

Animals feed on plants.

This bird is eating a flower.

Meal time

Put some nuts and seeds outside in winter. Which animals come and feed?

This squirrel
is eating
a nut.

Cows feed
on grass.

Plants help us

Plants give us many things. Trees give us wood.

Plant-made

Look around your house. Can you find three things that are made from plants?

Paper is made from wood.

We make
cotton from the
seeds of the
cotton plant.

We use flowers to
make soap smell nice.

Glossary

Fruit
The part of a plant that contains the seeds. We eat many types of fruit.

Leaf
The flat parts of a plant that grow out of a stem.

Nut
Dry fruit with a hard shell.

Petal
Colourful parts of a flower.

Root
The part of a plant that grows under the ground.

Seed
The part of a plant that will grow into a new plant if it is put in the ground.

Shoot
The first part of a plant you see when it starts to grow.

Sprout
To grow new parts.

Stem
The part of a plant that grows above the ground and puts out leaves.

Trunk
The woody stem of a tree.

Vegetable
The part of a plant that we grow for food.

Grow some beans in a jar

1. Find a clean jam jar and fill it with cotton wool. Add some water to the bottom of the jar.

2. Poke three or four bean seeds between the cotton wool and the glass. Put the jar in a warm place.

3. How long does it take for the roots and shoots to appear? Which way do they grow?

4. Turn the jar on its side and leave it. Which way do the roots and shoots grow now?

Index